Mirrors Full of Coats

Mirrors Full of Coats
Grief in E-minor

Autumn Lindsey

Copper Xylophone Publishing Co.

Copyright © 2021 by Autumn Lindsey
All rights reserved.

No part of this book may be reproduced in any form or by any electronic or mechanical means, including information storage and retrieval systems, without written permission from the author, except for the use of brief quotations in a book review.
Cover Design: Autumn Lindsey

Paperback Edition ISBN: 9781735053639
Digital Edition ISBN: 9781735053646

Preface

This book of poems contains my heartache, my tears, and ultimately my memories of a person I dearly loved who suffered from Alzheimer's, my grandma Rosalie. These were written as a way for me to not only process my grief but to also celebrate her memory. My grandma was an incredible pianist who had a passion for music and shared that passion through teaching the piano to others, including myself.

My hope is that these pieces might serve as words of understanding to those who have also lost a loved one to Alzheimer's. To those who know the hurt of mourning someone who is still here, to those who know the pain of becoming a lost memory of someone they love.

To the ones who mourn the living

This day is all that is good and fair. It is too dear, with all its hopes and invitations, to waste a moment on the yesterdays.

— Ralph Waldo Emerson

Contents

1. Broken Keys	1
2. The Sunroom	3
3. Our Finest Symphony	4
4. Fleeting Whispers	5
5. Return	8
6. Shiny Red Nails	9
7. Mirrors Full of Coats	10
8. My Heart was Home	14
9. A Love not Forgotten	16
10. Let Go	18
11. E-Minor	19
12. A Spell for Grace	22
13. The Cactus Bloomed	23
14. Dancing in the Hope of Mouring	24
15. Dry Your Eyes	25
About the Author	29
Also by Autumn Lindsey	31

part one

There is a storm within this world

A dark wave pulling me into the depths

of her choppy black waters

Broken Keys

Music echoed through the walls of her house.
Vibrating string and hammer,
as her fingers danced across the ivory,
 when the sun was warm and the flowers bloomed.

Her garden housed fairies with secrets of adventure who
paused their games to hear her play.
Even the moon sang along as it rose from the horizon
each night to Violet's song.
And the stars would wink, and dreams were safe.

The old clock would tick and tock keeping rhythm
through the night while she slept until morning when the
red breasted robin and blue birds would wake her with
songs of their own.

A new day to begin, a new song to be played.

Day in and day out her ivory keys would sing her joy into the world.

Until one day the sun grew cold and the moon forgot to rise.

And the stars burned out

and dreams were no longer safe.

The old clock lost its spring and the fairies and birds were eaten by starving cats, who laughed as they snapped the wishbones in two.

"Wishes- ha!" They'd scoff.

And Violet would hide under her broken piano to take shelter from the rain

that never

                    stopped

                                      falling.

The Sunroom

Grey aggregate beneath my feet
and flowering waterfalls flow from baskets
hanging above me in the sunroom
My fingers run along long filigreed
stems of the ferns
Innocently stripping leaves from the stems,
before I knew better

The sunroom,
a jungle of green arms reaching
as far as the propagated
lined window sills of her kitchen
Continuing the legacies of her
Christmas cacti and geraniums

> They say plants represent wisdom
> Where there is wisdom there is life
> There was life in the sun room

Our Finest Symphony

D, G, C
    The last three notes we played together
    Beautifully in sync
    Teacher and student
    Master and apprentice
    Grandmother and granddaughter
    D, G, C
    A duet of the heart, no, of the soul
    Connected forever by these three last notes
    D, G, C
    Beautifully in sync
    Our finest and final symphony
    Forever the song of my heart
    A now silenced memory
    D, G, C

Fleeting Whispers

You remembered me.
Well, not me, as I am now— but as that tiny baby you
carried upon your chest, as the little girl you loved so,
when you were younger and the memories flowed free.
Now, I am but a stranger.
A darkened face simply sitting atop a figure.
Nameless and unknown,
you look at me through vacant eyes.
But I see it,
As if some part of who you were searches helplessly for
files no longer existing in the fabric of your mind.
Until you find it (the old you that is)- a glimmer of hope.
Familiar faces from long ago of a little girl and the baby
you carried upon your chest.
And for one fleeting whisper of a moment
you remembered me,
and how you loved me so,
when you were younger and the memories flowed free.

part two

The familiar icy sting seeps into my bones

Searching for a place to settle

A place to set anchor within

Return

You came back last night.
As you were when I was young.
And papa was happy, I've never seen him so happy.
And I wondered if you had something to say.
Until I realized you said it in your return.
A moment of you, as you were; when I was young and
you could remember.

Shiny Red Nails

The sharp floral scent that was always too strong lingers at the memory of her
    The click-clack of shiny red nails on piano keys echo through my mind
    All a warm
    All welcome
    Even though it brings with it a deep sorrow
    A hurt unable to heal
    Fate itself cannot take away the sharp floral scent and click-clack of keys
    Nor do I wish it to

Mirrors Full of Coats

Tears fill her fearful eyes as panic-stricken words of a soul held captive stream out in incoherent cries for help.

She pleads for forgiveness and begs for mercy.

"I don't deserve this." She says, wiping her nose with a tissue from her pocket.

She hoards them now. Taking them from anywhere she can find; restaurants, bathrooms. Long gone are the days of collecting spoons and straws.

I miss those days.

"I love you so much," she says sobbing. *"You've been with me through this for so long. And I'm so sorry."*

I place my hands alongside her cold, wrinkled cheeks and

look deep into her glossy eyes holding back tears of
my own.
Certain if I let one fall the rest will follow and never stop.

"You have nothing to be sorry for," I tell her.

And then she's gone.

The one holding her captive returns and takes me on a tour of the house, showing me the rooms of bread and mirrors full of coats.

part three

But the song of my soul sings out

Stronger than any storm

For I have weathered so many before

My Heart was Home

I was there with you, last night, in your kitchen.

I know because I kept comparing how much my new kitchen reminds me of yours.

How the dark brown grout makes the most perfect grid around each and every cream and yellow marbled tile.

The yellow, like little bubbles of chicken soup, lying within each square.

This is the place you always seem to meet with me.

We were making soup, actually.

Stone soup, with all the ingredients laid out before us on the small counter.

All with nice, individual labels on their own individual containers.

Easy to keep straight, organized, not anything like you or I.

The counter in my kitchen is slightly longer, but the similarities are still an undeniable match to yours.

Perhaps I just want it to be that way.

And you—

There you were talking with me, just as we used to talk over the years, in your kitchen, making food.

And my heart was home.

Even though it lasted only a minute—

my heart was home.

A Love not Forgotten

He couldn't see the amounts on the bills with his eyes, but she could.

And although she couldn't remember what amount the bills said after she read them, he did.

He was her memory and she was his eyes.

She may not have known where they were driving, but he would navigate the familiar areas with what little sight he had as she drove and they always got to where they were going.

Then, as time went on as time does, the car disappeared from the garage.

The letters she tried to read on the pages he could not see, ceased to form themselves into proper words.

Still, he was her memory, even though she no longer could be his eyes.

When the world around her darkened he became more than her memory, he became her light.

When everyone turned into a stranger, she still called for his familiar hand.

And when words could no longer be spoken by her, his name still would whisper from her lips.

Her only light in a sea of darkness.

His only love in a world without sight.

And when the day came her eyes, that were once his, finally blinked their last blink, he knew he would forever hold her memory tenderly within in his own. And although their love was blind it was true, and true love is never forgotten.

Let Go

Please let go
> Of the pain
> The loss
> The forgotten
> -Let go

E-Minor

I long for the pain each note brings

Plinking like rain onto my broken heart

As your memory waltzes in and out

1, 2, 3- A tear tries to escape

I stop it

Bottle it up for a later time

A time more fitting than now

4, 5, 6- I hold the E-minor in my hand

As the sting of each dissonant chord pierces my tender skin

From the song you left behind

And keep it forever as a reminder of what it's like to feel

The pain of each note on my broken heart

Each beautiful, beautiful note

part four

My skin warms as I rise to the surface

Rays of sun decimating the darkness

slipping into the peaceful rest of night

Ready for whatever may be in the days to come

Knowing I am strong

Knowing I am enough

A Spell for Grace

Close your eyes and rest your head
go back to when you first began

Your mother's touch will soothe all fears
will hold you close and wipe your tears

Go find that place where you feel safe
where you were loved with warm embrace

And I'll wait here
till you return
however long it takes

And if you don't come back at all

I'll wish you love and grace

The Cactus Bloomed

The cactus bloomed and I cried
    She can't remember anymore
    So, I remember for her
    Things like birthdays and how much she loved when her cactus bloomed
    How it would brighten her sunroom with its pink blossoms each November
    Reminding us of the beauty of life in the midst of dying leaves
    as the world prepares for winter
    as the days grow darker
    The cactus bloomed and I cried
    because her cheery pink petals hold the memories of a woman who can no longer remember
    A woman I love dearly, who loved this cactus and its bright flowers in the fall

Dancing in the Hope of Mouring

The blossoms have faded,
your time has come.
Waiting for me under the bright Yule
*   moon we said our goodbyes as you*
*   drifted away on a moonbeam.*
Though sorrow weighs heavy in the thick
*   air of morning,*
a new season begins while the moon lays
*   to rest with fading stars under a*
*   blanket of indigo.*
And as the dawning of the first winter sun
*   crests over the hilltops,*
I see you dancing in the gleaming hope of
*   morning,*
Smiling bright
— Joyfully free

Dry Your Eyes

Dry your eyes, dear one, for I am at peace
    Resting with the ones who have gone before
    And though I am away from you in body
    I will always be with you in spirit
    A delicate melody drifting on a summer's breeze
    A gentle whisper in the dark of night
    May you hear my voice
    May it comfort you
    May it bring you strength

mended melodies

My tears fell less and less
at the mention of your name
As each week passed

Until one day the rain ceased
and the sun's soft rays broke out through
the heavy clouds shining on a single rose

And I found I was smiling
And my heart was light
At the thought of you

About the Author

 Autumn Lindsey lives with her husband and three kids in a deep, dark, magical forest in Northern California. Fluent in typo and fueled by caffeine, she writes Women's Fiction with characters that bite. Her debut novel Remaining Aileen is available through all online book retailers.

She is also the co-founder of Writer Moms Inc, a community for moms who write.

Also by Autumn Lindsey

Remaining Aileen

All That Remains

www.ingramcontent.com/pod-product-compliance
Lightning Source LLC
Chambersburg PA
CBHW060345080526
44583CB00014B/1066